WOMAN SONGS

Ruth de Menezes

CLAREMONT PRESS

Thousand Oaks, California

WOMAN SONGS

Published by Claremont Press, Post Office Box 4976, Thousand Oaks, California 91359.

★   ★   ★

Library of Congress Catalog Card Number: 82-71678

de Menezes, Ruth.
Woman Songs.
Westlake Village, CA: Claremont Press.

ISBN 0-941358-01-1   (hard cover)

ISBN 0-941358-02-X   (soft cover)

Printed in the United States of America

ACKNOWLEDGEMENT

Many of the poems in this collection have been previously published. We acknowledge with appreciation the courtesy of the editors of *Magnificat, Voices, Visions* and other magazines who have given permission, written or implied, for certain poems to be reprinted.

For you who open these pages —

This book is for you.
These are your songs . . .

SONGS

I   *Andante espressivo . . . con amore*

If I go a secret way . . .

FOR A YOUNG GIRL

If I go a secret way
 With silent lips and guarded eyes,
Think not that grief has stopped my throat,
 Think not that now no laughter lies
Beyond my eyelids' heaviness.
 Happiness flowers in this disguise,
And the four, solemn seasons bring
Joy too holy for heralding.

Remember, spring has ever come
 Unseen, unheard,
And all the ardent roses bloom
 Without a word.

LINES ON JEANNE D'ARC

You know her as a maid who did God's will—
A shepherdess who laid her distaff down
And rode to save a country and a crown,
Leaving her sheep alone upon the hill.
But though she was a soldier swift to strike
And rout the foe, I think at close of day
She was a girl who faced the stars' array
With tears, and wondered what a kiss was like.

Under her steel, Jeanne must have been most fair;
Her young heart must have held a girl's shy dreams. . .
Surely she liked the gowns she saw at Rheims,
And gallants laughing with the ladies there . . .
You know she gave her life for France's good;
I think she gave far more — her womanhood.

THREE CINQUAINS

SPRING

Tall, white
Gladiolas
Lifting their heads to the
April sun are like young choir boys
Singing.

PLEA

Hasten
Our marriage, lad;
Love is like brewing tea:
It will grow bitter if it waits
Too long.

WARNING

Beware
Of illusions
Woven at dusk; even
Cabbages are glamorous in
Moonlight.

FOR ONE WHO WOULD GO

Beauty and wisdom may be strange to me,
But with their fair disciples I have learned
What Helen knew when haughty Troy was burned,
What Sappho wept beside an ancient sea.
Deirdre in goodness, Guinevere in guile
And desolate Isolde in her grief —
Each learned the gesture, exquisite and brief:
To say goodbye — to say goodbye, and smile.

I know the worth of pride too well to stay
You with my lifted hand or shadowed voice
Even a moment; you have made your choice;
The gate is wide for you to go your way.
(My dear . . . Although I say goodbye and smile,
I shall be waiting for you . . . all the while . . .)

NO GIRL CAN BIND

No girl, however ethical and wise,
Can bind the heart that flutters in her breast.
Try as she will, she never can devise
Chains that will hold it tranquil and at rest.
Discipline as she may her lips and eyes,
Measuring every thought and every word,
One day she wakens, finding in cruel surprise
Her heart has flown with the swiftness of a bird.

And she will learn in anger and in pain
Ten thousand Aves will not bring it back again.

LOVE HAS STRANGE WAYS

Love has strange ways.
His spirit is most exquisite and fine,
 And I have known him countless days on days.
His heart has walked the roads traversed by mine.
 His mouth was made for girls to sing about,
And I have tasted the delight thereof.
 I am his true betrothed, but still I doubt
  If this be love.

Once, long ago,
A boy's blue eyes looked briefly into mine.
 He went his way, and I shall never know
If his young soul is exquisite and fine,
 How kindred is his heart, how sweet his kiss,
But wild thoughts of him burden all my days.
 I have learned little, but I have learned this:
  Love has strange ways . . .

THE SWALLOW

If I should follow
Sometimes in strange paths
You will not follow,
Oh, never fear.
Each night, as the venturous swallow
Turns back to her nest,
I shall come home
To your beneficent breast,
Most dear.

SIX WOMEN

Cleopatra, slim and wise,
Won a kingdom with her eyes.
Crowned with musk, ringed with myrrh,
Half a world belonged to her.

Sappho fashioned songs so sweet
The very gods knelt at her feet.

Joan was gallant; Joan was brave.
Bless the ashes in her grave!

And Helen of the fateful star
Thrust two nations into war,

While Celtic Deirdre's lovely face
Made Ireland an enchanted place
And the hearts of men grow wild.

Nancy Lincoln had a child.

Of these women lost in dust,
Whose bones lie the quietest?

Ruler, singer, soldier maid,
Sweet betrayer, sweet betrayed,
Mother of the burning hearth—
Who rests easiest in the earth?

Only the waving grass can tell
And the green grass never will.

But when I search for wood at dusk,
Forgotten are the myrrh and musk;
Forgotten, Rome; forgotten, Tyre,
And lips too bright and hearts too wild.
Against the night I build my fire,
And as I watch the golden flame,
I remember with a dream,
Nancy Lincoln had a child.

The kingdoms of the three fair queens
Are scattered now with Sappho's songs
And Joan's brave cause was burned with her.
O broken jewels! O vanished myrrh!

Imperial Sappho, Helen, Joan
And Cleopatra on her throne
Are dead with Deirdre the beguiled.

Dead are Nancy and her child.

INTELLECT

The body's fairness is not my first delight
    Although I have praised its strength and grace by day
And slept with its friendly beauty in the night.

    I have not heeded the body hard at play
Nor the precision with which the long limbs move
    Along a watery or a snowy way.

It is the mind's lean shape and color I love,
    Its bright dexterity that gives me pleasure,
And often I have rejoiced to see it rove

    Meadows of meditation at its leisure,
Challenging sometimes opinion's stream close by,
    Breasting its currents with a splashy measure.
And then what joy to watch this intellect try
    Its frosty skill on logic's treacherous ice
And with many a leaping and curvet fly

    Along a path invisible but precise.
Easily can I perceive and set at naught
    The snare that the lips or a glance can devise

But in the dominant mind's triumphant thought
I am held as with hands — I am hopelessly caught.

HIS ANSWER

"This April night you vow I am most fair,
And that your love will outlive time and space,
But still I lift an apprehensive face
The while you kiss my flower-scented hair;
For Age must also call on me to woo,
And he will win what you so worship now:
Bright hue of lips and eyes, the smooth, white brow . . .
When beauty goes, will your deep passion too?"

"Dear one, I also love your heart and mind,
And that fair soul which none shall win but I;
Yet, if my coxcomb rival makes you sigh
Despite this truth, grieve not, for you will find
I cannot look upon your aging face
Because we lie in such a close embrace."

MARRIAGE

In varied ways both fabulous and sweet
Life fosters many loves and joyfully
Marries the blossom to the honeybee
And weds the rich earth to the golden wheat.
The monk who kneels in his austere retreat
Is husband to his prayer; sagacity
Is subject to the sage; in ecstacy
The lover makes the breathless bride complete.

These are the fortunate and enraptured,
But sighing, each could tell you if he would
That the still, secret heart of womanhood,
Of thought, of flower, remains uncaptured.
No love, however much desired and dear,
Can find its perfect consummation here.

LOVE

Many a lover to her love has said
In the sweet darkness of their honeymoon,
"Embrace me once again, beloved, for soon —
So swiftly pass the years — we shall be dead,
Translated to that land where none may wed
And where however we may importune,
Kisses are contraband, and a sad rune
Divides these two whom once love comforted."

Such grief must make the angels smile, for she
Who enters Heaven will soon discover
The terrible raptures of one Lover
And love exalted to Infinity;
While earthly love, star-constant and star-bright,
Is lost as is a star in morning light.

THE SPLENDID LOVERS

The women of a lesser love may find
A rare delight in fleeing from a kiss,
Happily certain that the fruit of this
Will be three kisses for the one declined.
I think the splendid lovers were more wise;
Dido, Francesca, little Juliet
And Deirdre never played the light coquet,
Feigning indifference with mocking eyes.

Each gave her love, as I give mine tonight,
In undissembled passion, well aware
There is no time for coyness with despair
And grief so near, for all too soon the light
Of ardent eyes will fail; the arms will drop;
The lips will whiten, and the heart will stop.

FOR MY SONGS THIS NIGHT

Words . . .
You are inconsequential as bright birds
Against the heaven of my love.

MORNING SONG

Come quickly, spring!
When the peach tree blooms again
I, too, shall blossom!

LOVE SONG

God knows I loved you, dearest, long before,
    But now, no longer compassed by the dark,
    With joy I see in you the patriarch,
Patient and strong, the tribal governor.
In loving Him, I do but love you more
    And in your face perceive all those who were
    His friends at Crib and Cross and Sepulchre.
You came with other shepherds to adore
    The Infant King; you turned from prayer
    In the great Temple to behold Him there.
You followed Him to the Tiberian Sea,
And in the Garden of Gethsemane
    Upon that tragic night, you drew your sword,
    Quick to do battle for the unarmed Lord.
Your eyes — Hebraic, tender, fathomless —
Looked on the Christ in His divine distress.
    Now in this western city I often mark
    The clear song of a Galilean lark,
And seem to hear, who never heard before,
Your vast flocks browsing at our very door.

Ah, Love, how blessed was my betrothal day!
    For like an anxious Father with a dreamy child
    Still far from home and easily beguiled,
He sent you to me to make sure I found the Way.
In choosing you, I chose Eternity!
    Blessed was that day! Dearest, let all our days
    Be like green palms uplifted in His praise!

II   Con colti di tamburi

Now from the hive of time this honeyed hour . . .

ON FIRST TREASURING LIGHT

Now from the hive of time this honeyed hour
By urgent hands is quietly withdrawn.
The stars are contradicted, and the dawn
Comes laggardly, and later wakes the flower.
Oh love, how many Aprils will unfold,
What griefs assail us, till we look upon
This hoarded separate hour that was gone
Before we knew what sweetness it might hold?

When in some far brave season peace has given
This singular hour to be lived at last,
May our lips taste, as in a spring long past,
Some golden portion of our present heaven;
And hedged by chaos, may we still recapture
The same bright beauty and the same wild rapture!

WAR

How many nights now have I paced the floor
With frantic fingers stopping my sad ears,
Striving to muffle a mad hemisphere's
Tormented voices that beseech, implore,
And with ten thousand sobs and broken moans,
Distracted prayers and loud, despairing cries
Unwittingly reproach my tearless eyes,
My bondless body and my unracked bones.

Now honor's a dishonor, while the pure
And lovely go defiled; one's own free breath
Stifles the nostrils while the good endure
Slow dying. Recalling another Death,
I grieve, "Poor anguished Christ! And thrice poor John
Who could not help the One he looked upon!"

LETTER FROM A SOLDIER

Last night I saw your evening prayers come over,
    My love, my love — my heart's delight;
I heard them murmur and I saw them hover,
    Dove quiet and dove white.

My courage and my steel are not enough
    For this unnatural and evil war;
Your prayers within this dark, my little love,
    Are my particular north star.

When we withstand the fearful bombings here,
    Battalions of your prayers companion me;
When I arise into this hostile air
    I see your prayers ascending gallantly;

And when I sleep, love in a far-off land,
I hold your prayers like flowers in my hand.

WHISTLES

Blackbird, blackbird
      Shrilling in the thistles
And slim boy piping,
      Hush your careless whistles!

Too often have the sirens
      Set my heart to drumming,
Shrieking in the startled night,
      Death! Death is coming!

These skies in some far day will be
      Pacific as before,
And rust will choke the sirens
      That blew so loud in war;

But no matter how merry,
      How innocent or small,
I'll never like whistles
      At all, at all!

LOVERS SHOULD DIE TOGETHER

May Almighty God
In His mercy grant the prayer
I murmur nightly —

When Death must enter
Our small dwelling place, let him
Take us together;

For if it happened,
Lad, that you alone should die,
Leaving me on earth,

None could console me,
And there would be no valley
That could hold my tears;

While if my spirit
Were the first to go, instead,
I would surely be

So sad in Heaven
Even the gentle angels
Could not comfort me.

III Delicamente . . . con desiderio intenso

All I have loved is mine forevermore . . .

POSSESSION

All I have loved is mine forevermore.
      Last winter's rapturous and perfect rose
Blooms now as sweetly as she did before,

      Nor is there any earthly wind that blows
That has the power to set one petal free.
      The hours die, but beauty never does,

And my far mountains and the far-off sea,
      Flowers and faces and music I have known —
A thousand things that have enchanted me

      Enchant me yet, and never will be gone;
      Because I loved them, now they are my own.

Along these streets, I tread a mountain trail;
      I watch the surf upon a distant shore;
Within my ears sound notes that never fail,

      And tender voices I shall hear no more;
While like some blossomy and hidden glen,
      My heart wears all the flowers the year once wore.

And you, the lost one, gentlest of men,
    Lover of poesy and sarabands,
Speak with me still, though now a citizen

    Of wild and inaccessible dark lands.
I hear your words, and while I dare not stir,
    You innocently lean to kiss my hands.

The clocks are silent, and the walls a blur;
The rose blooms on, and you are as you were.

A SONG REMEMBERED

Just now, as many years ago, I heard
The rapturous singing of some little bird
Embroidering the evening with delight,
Crying a crystal welcome to the night.
How happily he flings his passionate notes
In patterned rhapsodies upon the air!
The startled heart leans eagerly to hear
The silvery melody of one who quotes
Precisely what his feathered forebears sang,
Making the summer ring as other summers rang.

The song is the song I heard
When another June was aflame;
But the bird is another bird,
And the girl is no longer the same.

THRENODY

Silent, mysterious, aloof
And delicately dressed in gold,
You dwelt within a crystal room
With gleaming water for your roof
And for your furniture, a stone;
And all who passed you might behold
How quiet was your way of life,
As tranquil, thoughtful, and alone
You slumbered, waved your fins, and ate,
Untouched by passion, greed, or strife.
Granting no favors, asking none,
You were content to meditate
And softly swim from sun to sun.

But yesterday a sudden change
Swept through your world; a passing boy
Who pitied you your Spartan role
Placed a great rose within your bowl,
And laughing, lightly wished you joy.
First, startled by the lovely bloom,
You fled and hid behind the stone;

Then, more assured, you warily
Approached your guest, admired her strange
Bright velvet fins, her long green tail,
Until at last, won over, grown
More used to beauty, you swam up
And reveled in her sweet perfume.

Alas! At dawn we found you pale
And pitifully still with death;
The flower that brought you happiness
Had robbed you of your golden breath. . .
And now I wonder, little fish,
As you were dying, did you wish
That life for you had always been
A bowl, some water and a stone? —
That you had never, never known
The glory of a scarlet fin?

Or were you rapt with wonder and delight,
And did you gladly die, as one who goes
Deeming death a trivial forfeit for a night
Of intimacy with a rose?

FOR A CERTAIN WOMAN — LONG AFTER

I do not need your brittle friendship now;
And though I tremble when your name is spoken,
Think not the reason is concerned with you.

The brave young soldier, home from distant wars,
Laughingly recounts a hundred battles
He engaged in, and tells off with winks
What leaders rode ahead, how great the foe,
And who fell prisoners and which ones died.
But when some stripling pipes, "And your first wound—?"
The muscles of his bronzed jaw flicker, and he pales,
Remembering not the swordsman nor the sword,
      nor yet the wound,
But the sharp, sudden agony of knowledge
That under this golden sun there is, in truth,
Malice, and pain, and death for youth.

Even so, I tremble to recall —
Not the bright heart withdrawn — but that hour when
In grief and loneliness I learned at last
There are blows struck by no visible hand
And subtle spears no armor can withstand.

SONNET FOR HELEN

I think that Helen was most beautiful
When she was old. Age brought a loveliness
That sharp, gay youth could never quite possess:
Her hands were whiter when grown dutiful;
Her breast, where once a shepherd's head had lain,
Was sweeter giving rest to some hurt child,
And those lips, long ago too bright and wild,
Were kinder as they kissed away the pain;
Her shining eyes were of a wiser blue
When they had learned the bitterness of tears.
She was so lovely, how I hope she knew
That although fairness goes when age appears,
Only when flesh is frail and faint with years,
Can the true beauty of the soul shine through.

THE QUILT

How smoothly lies your quilt upon my bed,
A timeless garden, beautiful with glowing
Flowers fashioned by your exquisite sewing —
Pink, lavender, blue, yellow and rose red.
How well you wrought with needle and bright thread
Until at last the lovely blooms were growing
That will keep babies warm when winter's blowing
Long after you and I, my dear, are dead.

So with your life: how patiently the years
Have pieced your joys and griefs and love's delight
Into a pattern quilted fine with tears;
Well it may be that on a nameless night
In a far time your life will serve to warm
Some child in some unfathomable storm.

COLLECTED LOVE

Eternity is a long time
And I passionately desire to spend it
Amid the ultimate raptures.
So I am busy — do not woo me with picture plates,
T-bills or painted thimbles.
I am impervious to gilded books,
Intriguing lithographs, Krugerrands and custom cars.
I know so well at the end
Even Gucci and Arden and the American Express card
Will avail me nothing.

It is true love I would collect.
Let me love without words,
Without demands or reservations,
In silence, remotely, the hundreds, thousands, millions . . .
And what cannot be seen or touched
And remains unnoted, unrecorded,
Beyond inventory or appraisal
Will be my pleasure, my delight —
Collected love.

IV   *Andante doloroso*

Now the abandoned blossoming
Of the wild plum is over . . .

BLOSSOMS

Now the abandoned blossoming
    Of the wild plum is over,
My heart is like a hunted hare
    That at last finds cover.

Hardy in so many matters,
    This my heart can never bear:
Boughs radiant with white blossoms
    Arched in the blue air.

PROCESSIONAL

There are no blossoms on the bough
Now.

Vanished the flowers, silent the sweet birds' song
And long

The death-dark path our weary feet must tread.
Dead

Are the dreams and the flowers, silent the song.

The rain falls sharp, the furious wind is cold
And we are old.

The strength and beauty of your girl are gone
Won

By implacable time. Our struggle's all uphill.
Still

As we go toiling through the storm, arm
Twined in arm,

I see a distant light, I hear a bell.
"Well"

It seems to say, "All will be well . . . Well . . ."

Take heart, my friend, my dear,
Our journey's end is near;

And soon, while others bow their heads and weep,
At last we'll sleep, my love;
At last we'll sleep.

TIME

O Time, you are a ruthless sovereign!
Up to this moment you have sent to me
Gifts of great richness and diversity,
But I perceive such lavishness will wane
And like all citizens of your domain,
I must submit to your gray alchemy,
Losing youth's color and sweet symmetry
And the bright gaiety the green sustain.

Much can you do with your persistent years
But I am not impressed; the spirit knows
That you who pity neither girl nor rose
Rule us but briefly. Give me age and tears!
I shall outwit you at the last and rise
With light laughter into the timeless skies.

DEATH

Breathless with wonder, transfixed with surprise,
I caught a glimpse of Death one Christmas Eve,
And my rapt spirit trembled to perceive
That here in this impalpable bright guise
Was perfect joy; the tongue cannot apprise
Such sweet delight, nor mortal heart conceive
His lightninged loveliness, but I believe
That all the stars of heaven were in his eyes.

So when my time for leaving life draws near,
When lover, friend and singing are no more,
Like some imprisoned lady sick to hear
The thunder of her rescuer at the door,
I shall wait Death, my cloak and gloves put on,
Watching the road, impatient to be gone.

VIGIL

At midnight there were four beneath this roof.
The doors were locked,
The windows closed against the dark.

At last the ancient clock
Spoke of the imminence of day
And lo, we now were three!

Without a word, without the opening of a door
Someone had slipped away . . .

A WOMAN'S ELEGY

Dreaming, I wandered from the country lane
    And there I found beyond a grove of trees
    A graveyard tended only by the bees,
Remembered only by the sun and rain.
Here blanketed by vines or leafy briars
    Slept those who loved and laughed long years ago.
    Between their beds, with reverent steps and slow
I made my quiet way, while cricket choirs
    Sent up a vesper chant. I bowed my head
    And when my little antiphon was said
In a far glade I saw the sumac's fires
    Burning a vigil light for someone dead.

Drawn by that silent glory, presently
    I stood beside the grave it heralded,
    And on its massive lichened headstone read
A woman's name, the year she died, and three
Words deeply carved: *"We loved her"* — that was all.
    Nearly a century has passed away
    Since those who knew and mourned her came to lay
Her body in this earth one early fall,
    But still those words so anguished and so old
    Tell to the stranger all that need be told.

With simple eloquence, well spaced and tall,
    The letters glimmer through the antique mold.

"We loved her." Only this. Long, long ago
    The hearts from which those broken words were wrung
    Returned to dust. Wild flowers bloom among
The grasses on her grave and roses grow
Around her name. A glossy vine secures
    A foothold in the path that none now tread.
    The woods crowd in about the ancient dead.
With flowers and rain and falling leaves the years
    Pass slowly by. Unvisited, unknown,
    She sleeps beneath her elegy alone.
Gone, gone are those who grieved, but still endures
    Love's testament, this little sigh in stone.

BELOW THE SEA

Fathoms below these blue and candid waves
in eerie waters where the water's weight
smothers all sound in breathless silences,
incredible creatures breed. Here among
    drowned gold,
forsaken ships, and mollusk covered bones,
float fish like mobile ribbons. Here
soft glowing things, all mouth and stomach, stretch
blind tentacles in quest of prey, and strange
bright colored animals fantastically like fruit
quiver and gleam upon the sunless sand.
Amid the dimness, seaweed grows, and stars
fashioned of cold persistent flesh
embrace the gutted rocks; while through the gloom
the giant octopus glides softly, dangling his dark legs.
Men cry aloud at wonders such as these! And yet—

there is a more mysterious Pacific
encompassed by one's own inscrutable skin.
Here pallid sponges quietly suck in
the strength of air, and streams of crimson
        silently engage
in trading weariness for that sweet strength.
Here swarms of red cells swim, and swift
white soldier cells patrol the crowded ways,
on guard against more subtle enemies
than deep seas ever knew, while brighter cells
combine and shift and once again combine,
and through their silent lightnings rule
a thousand nimble lanes.
Amid the dimness, coral colored walls
contract without a sound, and membranes make
shrewd choice of sustenance, while through the gloom
dark blood keeps pace with a moon it does not know,
and in a magic stillness, the pale fronds
of feathery tentacles give invisible seeds
a purpose and a destination.

More beautiful and strange than any gold,
Within such depths as these are domiciled
in mystery that bespeaks diviner seas —
a song . . . a dream . . . a child . . .

V   Moderato molto capriccioso

I have only one string to my lute, love . . .

LAUGHING SONG

I have only one string to my lute, love,
I have only one string to my lute.
So play a roulade on your flute, love,
For I've only one string to my lute, love,
I've only one string to my lute;
And you know so well what it is, love,
So bend your warm lips to my kiss, love,
And I'll sing you my song once again, love.
     In rapture, in pain,
     In sunshine, in rain,
I'll pluck the one string of my lute, love,
     Again and again and again.

HEAVEN

Since Heaven is a perfect place,
Outside of Time and unaware
Of all the priorities of Space,
What odd delights await us there!
For I may always be with you
But you need never be with me
Unless you wish — and if you do —
Oh sweet, oh gay uncertainty! —
I hope you'll think, "I see her hair,
Her hands and face, but is she here?
Is my beloved in truth with me,
Or does she only seem to be?"

Ponder long, sir; ponder well,
But ask me not — I'll never tell!

TWO SONGS OF PRAISE

I

Praise God for all delightful things —
    For lilting music and delicious laughter,
For one love's lovely whisperings
    And the long kisses that come after.

Who loves delight loves Him Who is delight
    And loves delight the most.
Praise smiling God and laughing Christ
    And blithe, capricious Ghost!

TWO SONGS OF PRAISE

II

Praise Him with finest velvet,
Praise Him with exquisite lace;
Praise Him with happy laughter,
With singing and grace;
Praise Him with joyful endearments,
A lovelier face.

Praise Him with chuckling children;
Praise Him with rapturous youth;
Let the flesh to its bones and their marrow
Glorify Him and His Truth.

Praise Him till sleep and its dreaming.
Praise Him each morning anew —
For He Who devised the bright spirit
Fashioned the body, too.

CONTEMPORARY PRAYER

Scotch Guard me against all kinds of dirt, O Lord;
Permanent press me with enduring love;
And after the great transition,
When the purgatorial waters have drained away,
Tumble dry my soul on the fast cycle!

VI   *Cantabile con molta espressione*

Suddenly out of the trees a cloud of birds . . .

THE SWIFTS

Suddenly out of the trees a cloud of birds
    Springs into the lonely sky,
Soaring and circling together with twinkling wings.
    In silence I watch them fly.

I see them wheeling with strange intentness,
    Moving in mystical circles through the light,
And I hear the delicate whispering of their wing beats,
    Hushed and remote in the ecstacy of flight.

Over and over they soar through the sky and turn
    And soar again — I wish I knew
Whom in the luminous air of evening
    They rapturously pursue.

DECEMBER MOMENT

This lovely thing must go unspoken;
Let not the quietude be broken.
It was, and I am sure you know
Who saw me suddenly wake and grow.
Strange and celestial, once this thing occurred.
So with these syllables I weave
A net to hold what I believe
And shall not put into a word.

NEOPHYTE'S SONG

Now with airy joy I know
Why the thrush and vireo
    Fill the skies with singing;

Wherefore the music of the linnet
Has such glad amazement in it
    And sets the whole wood ringing.

The same bright rapture in my soul
Shakes the feathery oriole
    And sends the wild lark winging

Up to the clouds to sing among
The notes that far church bells have rung;
    And every small bird swinging

Within the shelter of some tree
Affirms his little ecstacy
    And sweetly dwells upon it;

While in the dusk the nightingale
With many a fluted, shimmering scale
    Contrives a leafy sonnet.

These singers long ago gave tongue
To all that I have lately sung.

Now girl below and birds above
Can sing together of His love.

PSALM

I brought a single flower to Your tabernacle, Lord,
And You presented me with mountains.
Before Your altar I offered you the cricket song of my
      adoration,
And the heavens were filled with the chanting of ten
      thousand angels.
I placed the candle flame of my love on Your table,
And You thrust the burning sun into my arms.

Who am I that You should overwhelm me with blessings?
For my spirit has the strength of a match stick.
My spirit has the depth of a raindrop
And the majesty of a grain of sand.

Lord, in times past my neck was of stone,
My knees were without joints; my heart was filled with pride.
But now I shall be like a cloud going before a great wind.

Blow me wherever You will, O Lord, and I shall go rejoicing.
Send me over the prairies and the hills;
Dispatch me to the deserts; enjoin me to traverse the seas.
Your will is mine. Your will is my perpetual delight.
Or in Your wisdom utterly disperse me
And with my ultimate breath I will cry out,
"So shall it be. Praised be the Name of the Lord!"

ZENITH

Now at its zenith burns my life's own sun;
The circle of my loving is complete,
And I go gowned in love from head to feet,
My pride struck down, my wilfulness undone.
Seek out no greater love, for there is none.
Love lights my eyes, impels my heart to beat;
I read my love, and it is love I eat;
With love each day is ended and begun.

Would I were Joshua so that I might
Command my sun to pause at my sweet noon
And let me love at leisure, who so soon
Will know the growing dusk and then the night.
Love well, my heart, and in far-distant skies
I may in some great dawn see God arise!

VII   Largamente . . . andante maestoso

Consider the cosmos of your body . . .

THE UNIVERSE EXPANDS FOREVER

Consider the cosmos of your body,
The constellations of your mind!

As a woman carries her child,
I cradled you deep in My thought
     from the remote beginning.
At last you sprang like a star
     from the dark womb of your appointed mother.

Hour by hour you grow.
Your light increases like that of a rising sun.
You are not today what you were yesterday,
And tomorrow you will be more.
You constantly become.

I have shot the fiery arrow that you are
And with terrible intensity you pursue Me
Who can never be attained.

Through infinity you rush toward Me,
The half glimpsed but never overtaken.

O arrow that longs to pierce My heart
     with love and understanding,
In your longing is My joy!

Come to Me, most marvelous of My marvels,
Growing ever greater as you come.

I, the unknowable Mystery,
Bless you as I eternally retreat.

THE POET AND THE ARTIST

RUTH DE MENEZES is a third generation Californian whose poems began appearing in print when she was just nineteen. Her work has been published in many magazines and anthologies, and she has been awarded a number of prizes.

A poem in her first book, *Thunder in Spring,* commemorating the death of George Sperry in a seamen's strike, was acclaimed by Robin Lampson, poet and critic, as "about as fine a ballad of the 20th century as we have yet seen."

P.E. Lewis evaluated "A Woman's Elegy" as "equal to anything written in English."

Ruth de Menezes is presently working on a third book, *You the Arrow.*

✶   ✶   ✶

GAYE LaGUIRE, N.W.S., was born in Michigan and earned her B.S. degree at the University of Michigan. There she became apprenticed to Marshall Fredericks, world renowned sculptor.

She now lives in California where she enjoys a growing reputation for her landscapes and portraiture. Her work is frequently to be seen in exhibits and she has won critical acclaim and national awards for her watercolors.

Dr. John C. Gowan has praised her for her "archetypal imagery and ability to capture the universal in her painting."

A NOTE
ABOUT THE MAKING OF THIS BOOK

The typeface for the text of the poems in *Woman Songs* is English Times. It was photocomposed at Get Set Graphics & Typesetting, Westlake Village, California.

The book was printed at the Graphic Reproductions Center, Newbury Park, California.

Illustrations are by Gaye LaGuire.